Scales and Tails

Meet the Crocodile

Suzanne Buckingham

PowerKiDS press
New York

With love to Croc and his wonderful wife, Ginger

Published in 2009 by The Rosen Publishing Group, Inc.
29 East 21st Street, New York, NY 10010

First Edition

Editor: Joanne Randolph
Book Design: Greg Tucker
Photo Researcher: Jessica Gerweck

Photo Credits: Back cover, cover (logo), cover photo, pp. 5, 6, 10, 12–13, 16 Shutterstock.com; p. 9 © Biosphoto/BIOS/Bios - Auteurs (droits geres)/Gunther Michel/Peter Arnold, Inc.; p. 15 © Patricio Robles Gil/Sierra Madre/Getty Images; p. 19 © Richard du Toit/Getty Images; p. 20 © Shaen Adey/Getty Images.

Library of Congress Cataloging-in-Publication Data

Buckingham, Suzanne.
    Meet the crocodile / Suzanne Buckingham. — 1st ed.
        p. cm. — (Scales and tails)
    Includes index.
    ISBN 978-1-4042-4504-4 (library binding)
    1. Crocodiles—Juvenile literature. I. Title.
    QL666.C925B83 2009
    597.98'2—dc22

                                                2008009265

Manufactured in the United States of America

Contents

Meet the Crocodile

Crocodiles are **reptiles** that can live on land or in the water. These fearsome animals have sharp teeth and large scales all over their bodies. They use their short, strong legs to crawl on land. Crocodiles are also fast swimmers with their long, paddlelike tails and webbed back toes.

Like all reptiles, crocodiles are cold blooded. This means their bodies cannot make heat. They often lie in the sun to get warm. Crocs move into the shade or take a dip in cool water when they get too hot.

Crocodiles live for around 50 to 75 years. Some crocs can grow to be more than 20 feet (6 m) long!

5

Here you can see the crocodile's long, pointed nose. You can also see the bottom and top teeth sticking out of its closed mouth.

What's in a Name?

The word "crocodile" comes from the Greek word *krokodeilos*. The first part, *kroko*, means "pebble." *Deilos* stands for "worm." The crocodile got its name because its hard scales are like small rocks called pebbles, and it has a long, wormlike body.

People often mistake another reptile, the alligator, for the crocodile. Although these two look alike, they have several differences. A crocodile's nose is long and V shaped. An alligator's nose is thinner and U shaped. When an alligator's mouth is closed, you can see only its top teeth. Both top and bottom teeth stick out of a crocodile's closed mouth.

SuperCroc

Paleontologists believe crocodiles have lived on Earth for over 200 million years. Some early crocodiles, named sarcosuchus, weighed almost 10 tons (9 t) and measured 40 feet (12 m) in length.

In 1997, paleontologist Paul Sereno found a 6-foot- (2 m) long **skull** of a sarcosuchus in Africa. Later, Paul and his team found more bones from this 110-million-year-old reptile. They decided to name it SuperCroc. SuperCroc's giant bones were cleaned and made into a display. Today, SuperCroc travels the world so many people can see this ancient reptile.

This model of SuperCroc was made based on the bones found by Paul Sereno and his team. That is one big crocodile!

9

The Nile crocodile is a large crocodile that can live in rivers, marshes, and swamps in parts of Africa.

Kinds of Crocodiles

There are 14 different species, or types, of crocodiles. Each kind has scales that are just the right shades of brown or green to **blend** in with its surroundings. The special coloring of each species allows it to hide from other animals.

The smallest crocodile is the African dwarf crocodile. It measures up to 6 feet (2 m) long. The Australian saltwater crocodile, which grows up to 23 feet (7 m) long, is the largest crocodile in the world. Some of these huge reptiles weigh more than 2,000 pounds (1,000 kg).

The Crocodile

A crocodile cannot close its mouth completely because it does not have lips.

Scaly Facts

- A crocodile can stay underwater for an hour before coming up for air.
- A crocodile's back feet have four webbed toes, but the front feet have five toes, which are not webbed.
- When food is hard to find, some adult crocodiles can last a whole year without eating.
- The hard scales that cover a crocodile's skin are called scutes.
- A crocodile folds its legs in close to its body so it can swim faster. Some crocs can go as fast as 6 miles per hour (10 km/h) in the water.
- Most crocodiles live in freshwater. Australia's saltwater crocodiles are able to swim far out into the ocean, though.
- If a crocodile gets scared, it may run as fast as 11 miles per hour (18 km/h)!

Home, Wet Home

Crocodiles live in **wetlands**. They generally stay near slow-moving water, such as a river, stream, or **swamp**. Most crocs live in freshwater, but some are found in water that is brackish. Brackish water has salt water and freshwater mixed together.

All crocodile species are found in warm parts of the world. Africa is home to the Nile, slender-snouted, and African dwarf crocodiles. The Johnston's crocodile and Australian saltwater crocodile live in Australia. Six crocodile species are found in Asia and India, while four others make their homes in North America and South America.

This Morelet's crocodile makes its home along the Corona River, in Mexico. This uncommon croc is in danger of dying out.

Crocodiles have the strongest bite of all animals. They cannot open their jaws easily if they are held closed, though.

A Powerful Jaw

A crocodile's **jaw** is very powerful. It is even strong enough to break bones! An adult crocodile can bite down with a force of around 11,000 pounds (5 t).

The inside of a crocodile's mouth is lined with about 60 to 70 sharp teeth. When one tooth begins to wear out or gets dull, a brand-new tooth starts growing under it. After the old tooth falls out, a new one is ready to take its place. During its life, a crocodile gets thousands of new, sharp teeth.

What Crocodiles Eat

With their sharp teeth and strong jaws, crocodiles can catch and eat many kinds of animals. Crocodiles usually hide underwater and sneak up on their **prey**. They sit or swim with only their eyes, ears, and nose above water.

Baby crocodiles like to dine on bugs. Once they grow bigger, young crocs eat small fish, crabs, and frogs. Adults eat animals such as turtles, snakes, and birds. Some adults are strong enough to eat pigs, monkeys, deer, and buffalo. Crocodiles do not chew up their food. They swallow small animals whole and tear large animals into pieces they can swallow.

This crocodile has caught and is eating a bird. Crocs will eat almost anything that they think they can catch.

These Nile crocodiles are just hatching from their eggs.

From Egg to Adult

A crocodile begins its life inside a small egg. A mother crocodile lays between 10 and 60 eggs. These eggs take 55 to 110 days to **hatch**. A baby crocodile opens its shell with a tiny bump on its nose, called an egg tooth.

A newborn crocodile is about 10 inches (25 cm) long. Mother crocodiles often carry their babies from the nest to water in their mouths. Mothers guard their **hatchlings** for about a year. After hatchlings grow into adults, they **mate** and lay new crocodile eggs.

Crocodiles and People

At one time, millions of crocodiles lived on Earth. Over the years, people have hunted these reptiles to make shoes, belts, and bags from their skin. Some crocodiles die because their wetland homes are destroyed. Today, eight crocodile species are in danger of becoming **extinct**.

Many people realize that crocodiles are an important part of nature. Several countries have passed laws to keep crocodiles safe. New crocodile farms have opened to supply the need for crocodile skin. In some places, certain wetlands have been set aside for crocodiles. By working together, people are helping save these mighty animals.

Glossary

blend (BLEND) To mix together completely.

extinct (ek-STINKT) No longer remaining.

hatch (HACH) To come out of an egg.

hatchlings (HACH-lingz) Baby animals that have just come out of their shells.

jaw (JAH) Bones in the top and bottom of the mouth.

mate (MAYT) To come together to make babies.

paleontologists (pay-lee-on-TAH-luh-jists) People who study things that lived in the past.

prey (PRAY) An animal that is hunted by another animal for food.

reptiles (REP-tylz) Cold-blooded animals with plates called scales.

skull (SKUL) The bones in an animal's head that keep its brain safe.

swamp (SWOMP) A wet land with a lot of trees and bushes.

wetlands (WET-landz) Land with a lot of water in the soil.

23

Index

Web Sites

Due to the changing nature of Internet links, PowerKids Press has developed an online list of Web sites related to the subject of this book. This site is updated regularly. Please use this link to access the list:
www.powerkidslinks.com/scat/croc/